Bathsheba Transatlantic

ANHINGA PRESS

Susan,
You are in some of these poems
and will be in more,
Love you dearly and am so
happy you are my friend

BATHSHEBA TRANSATLANTIC

SARAH WETZEL

Here's to poetry and wine
and beautiful clothes

2009 Philip Levine
Prize for Poetry

Selected by
Garrett Hongo

ANHINGA PRESS
TALLAHASSEE, FLORIDA 2010

Cover art: *The Poets (Lilith Series),* lambda print, 140 x 99 cm,
      by Lisa Holden (www.info@lisa-holden.com.)
      Courtesy of the artist and Contemporary Works/Vintage Works
      (www.contemporaryworks.net).
Author photograph: Eli Atias
Cover design: Carol Lynne Knight
Design & typesetting: Jill Runyan
Type Styles: titles and text set in Minion Pro

Library of Congress Cataloging-in-Publication Data
Bathsheba Transatlantic by Sarah Wetzel – First Edition
ISBN – 978-1-934695-21-0
Library of Congress Cataloging Card Number – 2010928797

This publication is sponsored in part
by a grant from the Council on Culture & Arts
for Tallahassee/Leon County.

Anhinga Press Inc. is a nonprofit corporation dedicated wholly to the
publication and appreciation of fine poetry and other literary genres.

For personal orders, catalogs
and information write to:
Anhinga Press
P.O. Box 3665
Tallahassee, Florida 32315
Web site: www.anhinga.org
E-mail: info@anhinga.org

Published in the United States
by Anhinga Press
Tallahassee, Florida
First Edition, 2010

for Ray and Carolyn,
my parents

THE PHILIP LEVINE PRIZE FOR POETRY

The annual competition for the Philip Levine Prize for Poetry is sponsored and administered by the M.F.A. Program in Creative writing at California State University, Fresno.

2009
Sarah Wetzel
Bathsheba Transatlantic
Selected by Garrett Hongo

2008
Shane Seely
The Snowbound House
Selected by Dorianne Laux

2007
Neil Aitken
The Lost Country of Sight
Selected by C.G. Hanzlicek

2006
Lynn Aarti Chandhok
The View from Zero Bridge
Selected by Corrinne Clegg Hales

2005
Roxane Beth Johnson
Jubilee
Selected by Philip Levine

2002
Steven Gehrke
The Pyramids of Malpighi
Selected by Philip Levine

2001
Fleda Brown
Breathing In, Breathing Out
Selected by Philip Levine

CONTENTS

Acknowledgments *ix*

ঙ

Delusion of Sand 1

ঙ

Rehearsing for Rockets 5
Shooting Turtles 6
Shelter 8
Israeli Bride 9
Holy Site 11
Poem for the Enemy 12
Through the Window 13
Heroine 14
Man Eating Horses 16
We Speak *Hebrew* Together 17
Year of the Bear 18
Open Wound 19
Assembly Line 20
Begonias 22
Courtesy in Small Eastern European Countries 24
Suburb Living 25
Tel Aviv Dead 26
Myth of the Israeli Man 27
This is Not About David Grossman 29
Fresh Water 30
Seven Station (Dis)Equilibrium 31
Infidelity 33
Plato's Desire 34
Suspicion of Insects 36
Gianlorenzo Bernini in Love, 1639 37
The Message 38
Living with Spiders 40
Untethered 41
Common Era 42
In Another Country 43

ঙ

BATHSHEBA POEMS
 Prelude: Bathsheba at Her Bath 47
 My Body Through Water 48

After Many Lamentations, Again a Wife   49
Someone's Son is Always Sacrificed   50
Covered in Ease   51
A Reflection Wavering   52
Shiva for the Girl   53
After Bathsheba: the Illusion of Goodness   54

ଔ

Girl by a Wall   57
The Difficulty Discussing Poetry in Israel   58
Two Views of the City of David   61
Letter in the Hand of an Illiterate Woman   62
Last Fallow Season   63
The Mystery of Tides   65
A Scent of Oranges   66
Field Guide to Mushrooms   67
Lavender Door   69
Every Night with Valentino   70
Sighthounds   72
Martini with Borges' Eyes   73
Hind Leg of a Dog   75
Stories of Snakes   76
Nirvana   77
Notes Taken at Noon to Birdsong   78
Their City   80
El Al Flight 8   81
Dreaming of Jesus   83
The Beauty of Holes   84
Everyday History   86
We Are Joyous   87
Looking for Jerusalem   88
Revenge   91
Milk Inside   92
This Place, For Now   94

ଔ

Notes   96
About the Author   98

Acknowledgments

Grateful acknowledgment to the editors of the publications where the following poems first appear, at times in earlier forms:

Barrow Street: "Delusion of Sand"
Boxcar Poetry Review: "Holy Site"
CALYX Journal: "A Reflection Wavering"
Cyclamens and Swords: "Fresh Water" and "This Place, For Now"
decomP: "Seven Station (Dis) Equilibrium"
Eclectica: "Milk Inside"
Folly: "Infidelity of Finches," "Gianlorenzo Bernini in Love,"
        and "A Suspicion of Insects"
Quiddity: "Shooting Turtles" and "Girl by a Wall"
Shampoo: "Untethered"
Two Review: "Two Views of the City of David"
Valparaiso Poetry Review: "Martini with Borges' Eyes"

I wish to thank Bennington College and the January 2009 graduating class for the creative support they provided during the two years I spent at Bennington working on an MFA, support which contributed to the completion of this book.

My gratitude, affection, and thanks go to the amazing Garrett Hongo, Tim Liu, Major Jackson, Ed Ochester, Henri Cole, Peter Campion, Miranda Field, Nancy Bryan, and Grace Schulman.

In memory of my mother, Carolyn Wetzel, for whom all these poems are written. In memory of Liam Rector who believed in poetry.

And with love to Danny, Maya, Oren, Keren, and Daphne.

BATHSHEBA TRANSATLANTIC

Delusion of Sand

It's possible to see and not to see it
at the same moment — I'm not speaking
of the way sand is no longer stone, nor

about the way I bury my toes in
to the suck and seethe of the edge until
I can barely free myself, but how

I invent water until its texture
no longer resembles the consequence
of clouds — still, the vegetable cloth worn
by the earth is not yours, not mine

yet one after another, we strip down,
race out in the thunder, *virga, in
visible, sandstorm shaped into drops,* embrace
each other's parched bodies, shout, *Rain.*

☙

And I told myself: When I come to the land
of the setting sun,
they'll give me a robe of purple,
a throne of gold.

And in that land I will find peace
for ever and ever
— That tale I made up myself.
That tale I was never told.

— Dahlia Ravikovitch

REHEARSING FOR ROCKETS

The most believable stories begin
in the Second Act. One day you wake up,
you're a roach, waving legs
in the air. Or the police take you away
at gunpoint, although you're sure
you've done nothing wrong.

The six-year-old girl under my hand squirms
as I fit a gas mask to her small face.
Behind a chemical toilet we've stacked
canned food and bottled water, crayons
and coloring books. We're practicing
for when the rockets drop.

I want to tell her a story. A man alone
drives a German automobile down
a dry dirt road. On the shoulder, a rusted Volga,
all the tires gone. There's a woman inside
scanning the horizon. She doesn't
turn as the man's car goes by.

From the radio, an old song plays
an incantation. The man and woman, *hmmm, hmmm,*
each under their breath. But it won't help them
find the hands and good eyes of their sons
and daughters. They won't even say
they're lost, if anyone's listening.

SHOOTING TURTLES

My husband, who spent two years guarding a hut
on the border, dreams the same dream.

In it, one of his soldiers steps from behind a barrier,
begins removing his uniform. *Sometimes I recognize*

the soldier, he says, *but I never stop him as he unbuckles*
his Kevlar vest, unbuttons his gray green shirt and pants to expose

his body to the dust and breeze. In the dream,
the soldier winks, then starts running

toward the enemy. *Some mornings,*
my husband tells me, *I'm sure it happened.*

⌉⌈

Once, when he was talking about the dream, I said, *Perhaps*
that's why so many artists depict Jesus stripped.

Some of us need to see the sinew and tissue
to be convinced of suffering.

Of whose suffering? my husband asked.

⌉⌈

We drank coffee in our garden
and he said, *Did you know*

Indonesians harvest sea turtle shells for jewelry and armor
so carefully the turtles live, burrow into the sand
until they grow back their shells?

I told him, *That's not true. A turtle without a shell is dead.*
It sounds plausible, he said, *shells are like fingernails or hair.*

No, I said, pinching my husband's arm. *Turtle shells are skin,*
as in human. Sometimes, even softer.

❦

I said, *I had your dream last night.*
About the naked soldier? he asked.

Yes, except I was on the other side of no man's land.
His bare chest in my crosshairs.

SHELTER

We renovated a house in a Tel Aviv suburb, enlarged
the basement for his children. We planted
bougainvilleas that would grow over the balustrade,
installed two bird feeders for blackbirds, hoped
for a squirrel. There's a green gate with a buzzer.

In the basement, there's also a bomb shelter. All houses
have them, some more spacious than others. The shelter
has reinforced walls, two steel doors. One of them,
the smaller, opens to a tunnel leading out to our garden.
It's in case of bombing and subsequent attack.

I wondered if the shelter could withstand a direct hit
as I carried boxes of books, spare blankets, and a small
table down, my favorite red chair that doesn't match
anything in the house. The boxes stacked neatly against
two of the walls. On top, I piled cases of bottled water.

To the children, who disappear into it for hours, the shelter
is a fort or castle, a secret passage for smuggling and treasure.
Once, I unbolted the door to the underground tunnel.
A line of dolls, one with black hair, one blonde, two of them
bald, sat at the entrance. All their eyes taped open.

Israeli Bride

Eyeing me in the rearview mirror,
the taxi driver says, *All airports are ugly*. This one

extends the length of a country. It's tense
that connects a person with a place.

Here I am, I'll be, and what makes it true
is that connection. On my map, which I know

is just a copy of a map, an arrow
points to a city with squiggly rivers running

in and out. Meanwhile, terrain keeps turning
in all directions. The taxi driver looks back

and says, *Well, you shouldn't have arrived
in August*. Outside, the landscape slips by

wrung out and wrinkled, all the battalions
of power line poles teeter

the edge of breaking. Then things
might have been different — the same map

somewhere else, a different city
with different squiggles. Just like the day

when Yair Kohen, the last leader of the last
of the Samaritans, brought

his bought bride from Siberia. He told her,
You're lucky, waving his hands

over his desolate village. For two days
his bride wouldn't open her eyes, thinking

the war must not be over. *You are*
a princess, he reminded her

so that she understood how the stone felt
in its stone wall. She said back, *I am a princess*

of rubble, as if the rest of the world
might not be ruined.

HOLY SITE

She tells the boy it's a water tower.
Concrete gray and green, it rises forty feet
on iron legs; egg-shaped, lank and warped, the body
curves like a turned bell. The roof rusted through,
it holds water, though only four feet deep, the rest
pours from the metal shell. No one remembers
the year it was built, but it's been standing there
a long time. At night, the boy hears the concrete
fall in wet chunks, a low wind whine
through its wide cuts. And he can barely
sleep. In summer, the boy swims
in its dark water. He goes all the way under.
She never stops him, though the water infested
with bird shit and invisible worms
will tattoo itself by winter in small red Os
on the inside of his wrists. And she doesn't
repeat the whispers: it's a messiah's cup, a chalice
disguised as a tower, the water tinged brown
by something other than iron. The barbed wire
fence, the steel barriers, the danger signs
all a hoax. So that no one comes. What good
would it do? Even if pilgrims appear
with an antidote, even if a single dose could cure
the fatigue and fever, it wouldn't be enough.

Poem for the Enemy

Before the firing squad we invent poetry

That we'll all return to where we're coming from

That the wrung hands might one day stop wringing

Even that the white wall will never come white

So we imagine the fingernails rose

That his hands all the way inside himself

We imagine them covered in white powder

That he carries them close to his chest

He throws soap shaped into small yellow Jesuses

He throws wall clocks and fluffy pink dogs

So that inside the taxi we'd been waiting for

So we erase him

Beautiful that war and all its figurines of carnage

Beautiful that war and all its toy guns cocked

THROUGH THE WINDOW

No rain for months.
It's a desert here so I drench

the plants daily. *Too much*, the Arab
who cuts my grass says, except

I like a smell of rot,
the lacquered leaves smeared

with black spots. I like midges
that swarm, surprised

to find stone steaming, flesh-colored
lizards, their hearts beating

against the living room glass, snails
the size of baby fists. I like beetles

and the feral cats whose eyes
stare into mine. Just like all those children

being driven around with no seatbelts —
we've got to build

the fence higher, the glass thicker.
Because one false move

and I'm telling you
it will all come crashing through.

Heroine

I throw the book I can't finish
to the floor — softly speak
to the insomniac frog who creaks

his own discontent
from a rainwater pond, *It's not enough* —

knowing already I'll be late
to the job I don't hate
though I never remember
at day's end

to whom I penned the last
urgent memo. Some philosopher,
probably from Wales where the weather
is always miserable,

wrote that the secret of happiness
is learning to love boredom.

Though I think he called it
tranquility. How can I be bored
when in Jerusalem

they're erasing Hannah Szenes
from Israeli schoolbooks

after new translations of her diary
revealed she didn't paratroop
into Nazi-held Yugoslavia
to save Jews but because she was tired

of ironing and folding other Kibbutznik's
underwear. *Only the men work
in the fields with the animals,* she wrote,
I've got to escape.

When the Nazis caught her
at the dropsite just before they
shot her, they reported she wouldn't stop

laughing. *But last week I secretly
milked a cow,* she disclosed, over and over.

MAN EATING HORSES

Gun shots ricochet from outside or a car
backfires. The dog starts to bark at the sounds
but my husband keeps reading
to his six-year-old daughter. She looks up
and tells him, *Read me a story with heroes.*

Last year, she watched a man hack
the head off another on the Internet
and today announced there's a one
in thirty five chance an asteroid *bigger*
than Israel will crash to the earth

in her lifetime. She hasn't yet learned
about probabilities — she's just in first grade —
so I told her, *If one comes close, we'll flick it away*
like dust. On the news, a boy a little older
than she lost a leg to a rocket.

It's no wonder I can't stop writing stories
about horses. They are frightening —
their wild dumb eyes, steel clad hooves.
I've seen them run. Yes, I'm one of those afraid
every horse coming toward me is at me.

From the bedroom, the little girl cheers
as a man with a hatchet chases a wolf
through the forest, rescues a family in the story.
My ear pressed to her door, the clamor
of hooves recede. Surely, I tell myself, horses
won't be coming for her.

WE SPEAK *HEBREW* TOGETHER

The little girl asks for a *knife*. I hand
her a small plastic bag for wrapping a sandwich.
She asks where are *her glasses*. I give her
scissors.

She shouts caw-caw
while flapping her arms, running
around the kitchen. I shout caw-caw
and come after her.

She asks how long I'll be in New York
and I tell her, *Two years*. She starts to cry. I hold
her close, saying, *Yes, oh yes*,
two weeks is a very long time.

YEAR OF THE BEAR

I may live to see the last white bear
extinguish, the polar plains it stalked

dissolve in the same slow way smoke
from faraway campfires moves

into an evening sky. Without sound
or obvious hurry. Perhaps a few

will continue for a short while
in big city zoos and laboratories

so that we can tell each other
that one day the ice sheets will return

and we can put the bears back —
caged bears who have forgotten

how to sleep through winter's long
cold months. Eskimos believe that bears

are the keepers of memories. Do you
remember last year in New York City?

— that dirty white bear that stared
into the face of your daughter

as she whispered, *I love you,*
her mittened fist pounding the glass.

OPEN WOUND

*It is a Jewish tradition to leave a small corner of your house
unpainted to denote the destruction of the Temple.*

Who needs reminders of what's been destroyed?
So I plastered the patch with spackling compound,
scraped its edges and lightly sandpapered it.

So I painted the smoothed surface red.
As if by year's end, the patch wouldn't turn
the color of scab, the edges lift and darken to black.

Because always in the distance, the leaden
noisily roiling Mediterranean, the incessant desert wind
they call *khamsin*, and the white of the afternoon sun.

Because buildings made of brick and concrete suffer
the same weathering as any rock surface.
You told me the incomplete reminds us

we've been assigned a chaotic world to finish,
as if I didn't know it's the spot where the rot starts.

ASSEMBLY LINE

I never knew their names, I announce as my husband and I
finish our morning cereal. The men

on the assembly line. I worked there three years as an engineer,
and never knew any of their names.

I timed the twist of their screws, the soldering
of hinges to raw sheet metal. I wanted to make their work
more efficient.

More efficient? he asks.
You know, eliminate men.

Does it make you feel better to talk about it?

ᘓ

Those who don't suffer are doomed. The idiots.
Speak for yourself, he says, pouring me a fresh cup of coffee.

I say, I suffer. I fear poverty. No one trusts
the poor anyway.

No, they're always asking for something.

ᘓ

From the archives at Auschwitz, there was a document
with red pencil notations. The notations chastise

the writer of the document for using the word
"gas chamber" — vergasungskeller.

Don't use that word. You're not supposed to use that word.
Don't use it ever again.

☙

I say, I remember three of their names: Daryl, Ray, and Jimmy.
(I made those names up.)

Don't feel bad, he says, setting the coffee pot
back on the stove. Back in the sixties, an experiment showed

the majority of adults, when instructed to administer 450 volts
of electricity to another person, did so. Repeatedly.

☙

But only after being assured
they wouldn't be held responsible.

Only when asked to continue. Only when told
the experiment required them to continue, it was essential

to continue, that they had no other choice,
had to go on.

☙

Some of the participants gave interviews.
One person said, now I see what I am capable of.

Did it make them feel better to talk about it?

BEGONIAS

My Arab gardener is a polygamist. He let it slip
    when I congratulated him on his sixth child,
his and his wife's, or rather his second wife's. His first

is expecting his seventh. In response, I muttered
    something about *so many* as he began kissing
his fingers, invoking a blessing from Allah.

I know the Archbishop of Canterbury
    made some remarks about accommodating
Islam, but lines must be drawn.

I mean, what would Gloria Steinem,
    Adrienne Rich and Alicia Ostriker have to say
about my gardener's diminutive harem?

They'd kick him in the balls, I'm betting,
    lecture him on the rights of women, the evils
of patriarchal societies. He'd go home

and divorce one of his wives, raise his girls
    to be doctors, his sons to marry one at a time.
On the other hand, *He works hard and seems*

honest, I've exclaimed to friends. Not to mention
    my begonias and roses, my bougainvilleas
and rakefet are blooming like they haven't in years.

After he finished kissing his fingers,
    his murmurings to Allah, he looked at me
full in the face and asked, *How many children*

do you have? I said, *None,* and could see
    from his eyes he was thinking the same thing as me.
I haven't invited him in for coffee since.

Courtesy in Small Eastern European Countries

The man at dinner with his wife and his daughter
who helped us decipher the menu turned out

to be an arms dealer selling weapons
to Algeria, Serbia and Nigeria. The wine

he recommended was Bulgarian and tasted
of ripe blackberry and peppers. He told us

the U.S. military stopped buying his merchandise
two years ago because his missiles didn't meet

its exacting standards. I felt slightly relieved
though found myself saying, *I'm so sorry.*

With a wink, he clasped both my hands in his
large one, told me don't worry, business

is booming. We laughed at the pun. My good
manners dictated I send him a note thanking him

for his advice on the food. He wrote back, *It was
my pleasure. If you have more questions, please*

call. I thought to ask about Serbia, tell him
the wine was delicious with an aftertaste of spices.

Suburb Living

I live secluded,
our house built by men
who some here call ants.
Shipped in from Thailand,
they carry loads till
the boss says, *Go home.*
Just like the neighbors
where there's no homemade
cake, quiet only
on Saturdays when
yard men and kitchen
renovations stop.
It's always too hot
in the streets. The dog
sleeps spread eagled like
me on days when I
can't write. Women, some
do work, ask about
children. I tell them
there will be none, by
choice, making me more
strange than not being
Jewish or someone
with gardening gloves.

TEL AVIV DEAD

All day Arab women on straw mats weaved
intricate caftans from gold silk, indigo thread.
That was the year I fell in love with Tel Aviv,

shopped the open air markets and believed
I was safe. No one cared that I'd wed
a Jew. But holy men on their mats conceived

techniques to build bombs and hide them in sleeves —
theirs out of cotton, ours made out of lead.
That was when I lived in Tel Aviv

afraid of Arab faces and places I couldn't leave
fast, afraid I'd end up in a hospital bed.
Young men (even women) on mats were deceived

by sermons and stories that called them naïve
for viewing *the enemy* with anything but dread.
That's when I began to loathe Tel Aviv.

There was no reprieve.
Only emptied markets, rumors of bloodshed
spilled on the mats of men and women who won't grieve
the day I leave Tel Aviv.

MYTH OF THE ISRAELI MAN

Please just stop with the story
about your father's three friends, Israeli soldiers
furloughed from the army who slipped over

Israel's ill-guarded southern border
into enemy territory, the old story
about how they walked forty kilometers

across Jordan's black basalt desert
to reach the base of Mt. Hor. Stop telling me
they just wanted to photograph

themselves, their arms around each other's
shoulders, big stupid grins on blistered faces
standing in Petra's two-thousand-year-old temples,

the robbed-bare tombs of some
long-dead Nabataean Arabs. Stop talking
about how they only drank water

because Israelis didn't learn to like alcohol
until the Russians showed up, about how
the three friends returned by night

by the same sand and granite route. *They
weren't just lucky*, you said. *It was 1966
the year my father learned to fear*

dogs, you said, *because they might
be carrying dynamite.* It was the year
of *Star Trek, Valley of the Dolls,* the year

you were born which was why
your father didn't go with them. Please stop
saying that if the Bedouins had found

the soldiers, they'd have taken them
hostage, shot them as spies. Stop saying,
Perhaps they did find them, at least

some of them. Please just stop
with the story about how
you would never have gone, and go.

THIS IS NOT ABOUT DAVID GROSSMAN

The famous author writes a story
about a woman whose son fights
at the front. The woman, who's begun dreaming
of deserts, leaves her husband

and a small cerulean pool
in the garden. She starts walking, believing
if she's not home to answer
the door, her son remains untouched.

Awakened in the middle of night
by military officers, the famous author
learns his youngest child, a tank
commander, disappeared

during a fierce battle that same
afternoon. A woman sits
at an empty bus stop between
nondescript towns. She's waiting

but not for a bus; the bus company
quit the unprofitable route
years earlier. There are no cars, no signs
of anyone. When asked how death

affects his writing, the famous author
said, *I do not speak of that.* In her
dream, the desert is flat and dry. She lights
everything on fire.

Fresh Water

Outside, a cicada casts off its shell, its face
five inches from mine as it separates
from its carapace, a creature grown too big
for its container. For a while, the cicada freezes,

trapped by tentacles of tissue fine
as surgical wire. A wound that slowly stretches wide
as the cicada greedily eats the flesh filaments
strand by tenuous strand until the carapace splits

and the soft body springs free, pale
as the inside of my wrist, as keenly vulnerable.

I wanted to feel new, to not be stuck, just like
the cicada discards its skin, a blackbird flies
blind at night lured by an idea
of clean water, a woman leaves one man

and lies with another. It's what I wanted,
isn't it? I raise my face to the fading sound
of an airplane crossing, the one I was supposed
to board, the one that an hour later

spirals into the sea. It's what I wanted —
not someone to say, *That could have been you.*

Seven Station (Dis)Equilibrium

1.
A man with a briefcase and unblinking eyes enters the train.
He speaks softly into his phone, *Do you mind if I go down on you?*
I move my skirt aside, make
room for him.

2.
Below ground, a real river quickens its pace, illustrates
the pattern in another material.

3.
Each piece of train falls and bends, a nail
holding the track in place (it can't fall farther or differently).
An engine pulls the passengers forward, a river
pushing them further.

4.
The river moves deliberately
through aquifers and underground lakes.
The blind white fish caught in the current
are hungry. They get on.
They get off.
They get on again.

5.
I press a hand to the shuddering wall of the train.
The man sits across from me.
He watches me.

6.
The train takes a breath, slow
as through a subterranean chasm.
A river then gives in to its wide open mouth.

7.
A man in blue uniform checks our tickets,
we who carry nothing suspicious.

Infidelity

Through the wall, a bush next door is begging
me to buy pomegranates, small bombs
more fickle than apples. As if it's already

winter when all the sinners in hell
are paired, all the lovers, when the bush's
extravagant flowers
                            the color of poppies
turn poisonous, the small brown finches
still yearning to carry the seeds

inside their bodies. The tree next door
flings its fruit at my feet, entreating me
to eat just a few. Yet if we can't speak
                                   of deceit
to one another, how can we speak of love?

PLATO'S DESIRE

No less a fixation than twelve o'clock's shadowless
body, more confusing than Hans Christian Andersen's
harpsichord maiden — in her anteroom the abandoned
shadow reads all the poetry ever written
to become human —

so we spend hours
explaining how it slipped away, the slant
of the sun, our bodies having given away more heat
than they could soak up. Or, we tell ourselves

it was a mirage, that for once in our lives
we arrived in time.

A man turns to his wife, each
on their mountain of cigarette butts, used
paper cups. *Am I your shadow*, he asks?

The woman shifts blind eyes toward the sound
of his voice. *You're my husband*, she answers.

But if she could have said yes!

So even Plato must have shouted his last evening
as he watched the cutout of his beloved
shimmy on the bungalow's white walls, the fire
singeing his arthritic fingers —

to go out without any guide

all the way through
the window and when I see you in the sun

wearing your threadbare blue cashmere sweater, a gold
cravat tied at your throat, I run toward you —

all the versions of ourselves
to which we are bound.

SUSPICION OF INSECTS

Whore, he shouts, pulling his wife's body down
the hall, thrusting her into the thick air
of summer. It's 2:35 a.m.
on Orange Street. She stands soaked in the glow

of the porch light, the milk thump of Angel
Moths like a pulse. She reaches up, unscrews
the bulb from its socket. For hours, she whispers
through the keyhole, afraid to ring the bell,

afraid to wake the neighbors. Mosquitoes feed
on her arm. To kill them would draw others
to the smell of her blood. As she cups the warm bulb
in her palm, she imagines a man in a serge suit

carries a vial. Inside it, she thinks, *the scent
of stagnant rivers.* The next morning, when he lifts her
gently from sleep, pries open her fists, both
hands are full of crushed glass and mosquitoes.

GIANLORENZO BERNINI IN LOVE, 1639

Human nature will not find a helper better than love.
— Plato, *Symposium*

You knew she craved another
when she flew to your brother;
her feet didn't touch the flagstones once.
That night, you slipped
through the window to watch
the bank of her body rise
and fall. You had carved in marble
that curve of an unlined cheek,
the mouth now trembling
with sleep.

But imagine the blaze of eye,
brilliance of the red
against linen
as your servant followed
into her chamber, slashed
her face with a razor. Beneath
even your chisel, stone
can't ape such agony.

What does one gain
from love? Some say immortality.
Your sculpture of that girl —
one can't forget her.
Or how desire can turn to vinegar.
As for the girl, banished
for her frivolous kisses,
she could see in the mirror
what love bares.

The Message

The trail through Al Madras was marked
by steps barely visible carved into the southern face

of what's technically not a gorge (think of water)
but a tectonic tear in Petra's mountain.

Far below us, miniature horses and, from this
perfect distance, people posed in front of a sextet

of red stone pillars holding open the chiseled façade
of Al Khazneh shrine, which in Arabic you said

means treasure. Although in two thousand years
of searching, none's been found. Holding hands

we could barely clamber over steep sandstone
escarpments to the place of sacrifice, to the caves

where houses of priests had been hacked from rock
that afterward became their tombs. The caves, I thought,

still seem lived in. You said, *When Moses*
led his brother into these caves, he didn't say

it was to die. Instead, Moses told him God
had a message. It was only when Aaron saw

the Angel, that he understood his younger brother
was a coward — I should have told you then

that what we feel most has no name,
just murderous angels' houses to graves the reason

I left you and the reason I came back — *which was*
the reason his followers despised him,
you said.

LIVING WITH SPIDERS

It's true what Pasternak said, *Most of us live lives*
of constant duplicity. As do the man and his wife living
on the edge of a forest who, when told
their home is infested
with Brown Recluse spiders,
refuse to move or have their home cleared
of creatures they've lived with for years.

Though if one of them
forgets, reaches a hand carelessly
into a box of old clothes, the recesses
of a closet, or rolls over onto a spider
in bed, and is bitten, the result
might prove lethal. Not that either would notice
such a small scratch

until the wound grew large, gangrenous
as when a tree rots. The only treatment —
excavation at the root. Still, the man
can't help staring at the scar
on the breast of his wife in the mirror
as she, stripped to the waist, washes herself
at the sink. Sometimes in the dark

like St. Thomas did to prove
the risen Christ was real, he puts a finger
on it, the white ridges
jagged and raised, until she shudders
in her sleep and he hears a scuttle
of spiders, the sound of one more leaf
adding itself to the pile.

UNTETHERED

In Brooklyn, a man's hand slips
from the ledge of a building
giving in to a craving
for matter. The same way
a cave

collapses
when the soluble rock
dissolves. The hum
of a dial tone. The phone pressed
to my ear. Most mornings
I put it down

because the time for begging
has passed. Listen —
I'm the sound of surf
with nothing
to smash against.

Common Era

*The Romans built a fortress knows as Castellum ten kilometers
outside Jerusalem. Most of its soldiers never returned home.*

In this land, you are forced to prevaricate

That the iron sword has grown too cumbersome

That the body big inside its metal armament

Her name Serafina, burning one or blue serpent

You Macario, blessed work spear, god is your oath

At the same sea edged by Ceaserea and Capri

Though underneath mountain chains, active volcanoes

You still search the horizon for that last *scapha*

Though the path disguised with strange clothes

Still tremble with the hum of bees rising

Wake with the sweet shriek of red Calaneet

You still think there is a way back, but there isn't

She sleeps, untouched skin mottled, long unstitched

Your eye from her yellowed embroidery

In Another Country

The word *alone*, difficult to pronounce
in another language. Nonstop flights, day
time talk at night, children who don't know my name.
Didn't I love you
          with my whole body?
     New York? Oh, Tel Aviv?
                    You said red flares
shot through water attract only dragon-
flies. Sharks here full hearted as chandeliers
but less reflective.
          I think I'm too far gone
to watch my shadow pass. I think I'm too
far gone to dress in beige.

            Alone in stone
cities, it's impossible to blend in.
      Myna birds loose, cuckoos laying their eggs
in the nests of crows. I can't spell the name
of the street I live on.
            Still I love the tree
that bleeds pink blooms yellow in every heat
wave. Photos of ice in summer, orange skies
in winter. I said I'd go anywhere
to be near you.
          Baby, where am I now?

ᏣᎦ

Those who remember me will know:
"She was lonely
and like every person she was woven from darkness and light
and there is almost nothing to remember —"

— Lea Goldberg

When David lay with Bathsheba I was the voyeur,
I happened to be there on the roof fixing the pipes, taking down a flag.

— Yehuda Amichai

BATHSHEBA POEMS

PRELUDE: BATHSHEBA AT HER BATH

After Rembrandt's painting, Bathsheba at Her Bath
(holding King David's letter)

how pensive she seems in Rembrandt's
painting, her body slumped on the stone seat,
limp hand holding

what, a letter —
how yielding her belly

it's the way a woman sits when she thinks
herself invisible

yet there's light pouring in
from the front of the painting, a spectator
throwing a shadow
into her —

otherwise Bathsheba's skin glows
unfloured, waiting
to be worked —

MY BODY THROUGH WATER

David sent messengers to get her, and she
came to him, and he lay with her.
           — 2 Samuel 11:4

      The moment: a pool
of lucidity. A relucent alluvion becomes
cleansing flood, the morning sun
a sibilance, its sound
a hiss from an animal shell.
Water churns
the start of a genuine river
while I, a sybarite dreck,
a limpet uncurling its edges,
am blurring.
      I watch branches break free
and surface, my body, softening
like the bank of a river clogged
with detritus. There are no mirrors,
his eyes darkening. Still,
I will be seen.
This rain-soaked seed that rots
breaks open.

AFTER MANY LAMENTATIONS, AGAIN A WIFE

I don't believe in God. I believe
in animal nature, in the shadows
of cats.

I believe in flint-gray
wives, in their husbands
and lovers. I believe in prophesy.

I influence clocks, set the pendulums
swinging and men
who are bombs ticking.

A teacher's words drift back: *You are just
a girl.* Street lights of cities flicker
and dim. Perhaps

but not the girl I'm becoming.

SOMEONE'S SON IS ALWAYS SACRIFICED

My Lord, you said my son would be King.
      — 1 Kings 1:15

Candent dusk,
            between lattices a red
Jerusalem where under each arch

a noose sways. Slowly I rouse to a rasp
of slipknots tightening, trap doors
                       collapsing.
Tonight,
        bless my mother. Inside
my body, her words rise: *from this*

no woman wavers. Some play hangmen, others
the hanged. I learned to ignite fire by watching

cats breed —
            how the friction of soft fur fashions
electricity, just as a whisper in the right ear

a poisonous ache.
           I won't waver.
To salvage what's mine — I'll reduce yours
to ashes.

COVERED IN EASE

If I'm a slave, then a slave
I want to be.
             Look at my filigreed slippers,
look at these lips. I'm not just
                          a woman
by quality, obsessed with ribbons.
I'm brutal as God, not
             limp
                          like his wings.

I'm a woman of my moment without
going into it. Look at my sisters.
                          No one
remembers their names.
             Just like that

sea out of sight, which is all that's left of
an earlier flood.
             No one smells it, only
debris.
      I'll go to my grave with six sons
to carry me
             in a box encrusted

with jewels. As a girl I knew just as much
although men will write,
             She's more turned now.

A REFLECTION WAVERING

once more the evening   grants amnesia from the heat
such a garish dusk   resembling old embers and ash
its light twists   shining through a rough-hewn prism
this maternal love   it's an instinct to drink
re-visioned   like a glass (wiped twice)
can appear clean   so what's lost? I think
no one tastes the bad water   when disguised with flowering vines
just as deep in a hidden grave   the real villain withers with time
last name forgotten   life transformed into story
and I'm just one woman   chasing a small boy

between my memories   God and my memories

chasing a small boy   and I'm just one woman
life transformed into story   last name forgotten
a villain withering with time   just as deep in a hidden grave
when disguised with flowering vines   no one tastes the bad water
so what's lost I think   can appear clean
like a glass (wiped twice)   re-visioned
it's an instinct to drink   this maternal love
shining through a rough hewn prism   its light twists
resembling old embers and ash   such a garish dusk
grants amnesia from the heat   until once more, the evening

SHIVA FOR THE GIRL

God of the sun and sand, of frail clouds
suspended, God of thorned acacias adorned
with shell colored moths, with crows, God of bare
feet and tanned shins, God of uncovered hair,
then of scarves, of tented bazaars, air bent
with smells of cumin and caraway, of villages
emptied and brooms made of straw, God of strange
instruments, of strings, of fingers, of the way
her belly shivered of its own will, God of the mystic
and false prophet, men flawed and their
followers, God of small Gods to whom she lit
candles, to whom she burned piles of green leaves,
God of the girl and grift and the grist
in the mill, God I cover the mirror, I rend
the dress from high neck to hem, God I paint
my breasts with black ash, wash my hands
of the grave, God of Jerusalem, her moon, her pale
see-through weight, God, comfort her, God
of her ghost who does not exist
but for God.

AFTER BATHSHEBA: THE ILLUSION OF GOODNESS

Through a window, I see my husband's six-year-old girl speaking again
with the refugee children. Her lips moving, our dog leaping

at a ball held high in her arms, the shadow of her small voice reaches
me in the late morning breeze. At least that's what I call them —

the girl with dark hair in a torn yellow dress, the boy whose right leg
is bandaged. It's the fifth or sixth time they've come.

She told me all they ever bring is a plastic bag filled with raisins
and an old black umbrella. Of course, they're transparent
to me, to the dog, which is why I don't ask about the boy's leg
or the umbrella.

Later, my step-daughter will request cinnamon cookies, little cups
of grape soda. *They can't find their way home*, she'll say.

I'll prepare the cookies and drinks, draw a map
that shows how to get back to their house. It's just on the other side
of the big eucalyptus grove.

She only asked once to go with them. I lied,
saying, *Children always find their way home, parents are waiting,
and their house has an enormous garden, a blue door.*

୪

I hate departure,
and I love the spring,
and the path to the spring,
and I worship the middle
hours of morning.

— Taha Muhammad Ali

GIRL BY A WALL

All day the fragile beauty of Israel's wall
poses like a young girl asking to be opened.

She's only twelve years old, the man
behind me says, but you must admit she looks
almost eighteen, says another.

As I gaze at the bar's widescreen TV, racy ads
competing with the evening news, I tell myself I'm done
defending this country to drunks.

So come girl, let's lie down in Israel's fields
like the bound wheat in those faded immigrant photos.

Our hands clasped, we'll watch rockets
weave through the cloud cleaned skies, wait
for small tremors. We'll pretend

we're dead. Then they'll see
how the puffs of dust lift and dissipate
with no relevance to what went on before us.

The Difficulty Discussing Poetry in Israel

What if there's a small blue house in Jerusalem
What if someone built the house illegally
What if a woman lives in the house with her six-year-old son
What if the house is scheduled for demolition
What if the woman's husband disappeared two years ago
What if it snows
What if snow can't slow the trucks crossing the city
What if people living along the road open their windows to see
What if the boy raises his face and smiles at that moment
What if he believes his father is good
What if the boy can't remember
What if men from trucks move a red table out of the house into the snow
What if bulldozers start in the garden
What if a man comes out of a house
What if this one man stands in front of a bulldozer
and raises his hand

ᏣᏍ

— I read your poem about the house.
   You portray the Israelis as if ...
      — Yes.
— There are two sides ...
      — Yes.
— Are you Jewish?
      — No.

ᏣᏍ

On the corner of Namir Street
where Philippe Starck
designed two forty-story towers stands
an olive tree. A man sits half

hidden in leaves shaking the olives
free. Below him, an Arab woman
looks up, open mouthed,
trying to catch one
with her lips. The silver lids
of the leaves flash
and wink but my car
won't stop.

ᛒ

— I appreciate that you answered. I worry
   about propaganda.
       — It's winter here, the beaches
           almost empty.
— When I visit Tel Aviv, perhaps
   we can meet.
       — To talk about poetry.

ᛒ

The hall in Haifa where Mahmoud Darwish spoke in Arabic
overflowed. A Palestinian poet, I couldn't understand
a word and so many wanted to see him. He said, *I thought poetry*
could change everything — could humanize — the illusion
necessary to push poets — to believe, but now I think poetry changes
only the poet. I read this later in translation. I believed him both times.

ᛒ

What if we open our hands and we look at them
What if invisible matter flows through our hands like air
through a window screen

What if we put our tongue to the mesh and taste sweet metal
What if we capture the flow in a cup
What if we fly a blue kite in its breeze or turn
a windmill
What if we slowly pour it on the ground

Two Views of the City of David

The black sack sails from an upper
window of a block house opposite
the viewpoint. I shade my eyes

with a hand observing the flawless
arc of its fall. The bag catches
on a small bush, dangles a moment

then tumbles once, twice, to rest
in a rocky ravine seething
with trash. White papers, freed, flap

through the air filling the bush's branches
with what seem twisted
birds. And I think of what's written —

a recipe, a letter, the first draft
of a story, some sort of explanation —
then thrown. Beside me, someone mutters

Arabs. A dark figure stands
at the window of the house looking out
at us, then turns. I almost wave.

Letter in the Hand of an Illiterate Woman

After Rembrandt's painting, Bathsheba at Her Bath
(holding King David's letter)

Black ink brewed from residue of oil
etched on papyrus thinner than skin
of an animal. The smell on her hands as if
something burns. She traces the pain taken

over each word, the geometrical rhythm
of angle and slope, curves like caves, their
mouths wide open, lines crumpled
and bent, lines crossed and combined.

He'd placed dots and dashes beneath
particular letters. She knows those marks
insinuate *ahs* and *ohs*
of speaking. She can't read, yet sees

each word has an edge. What kind
of man sends a letter to a woman
who can't read it? What kind of man paints
her portrait holding a letter? —
                              Revealing

the illusion
how carefully she keeps turning it over.

Last Fallow Season

I won't promise to tell
when things turn worse —

last summer our old olive tree bore
no fruit and I didn't see it

until this week when the dog started
bringing olives just-fallen inside.

My dog will carry an olive for hours
until the hard ball turns to pulp. Then

he'll leave it. Among the roots
of the tree, I found centipedes long

as pencils, white moth flurries, fragile
lace wing flies who lay their almost

invisible eggs on the smallest leaves.
Once, I found a toad whose silvery skin

blotched green seemed a medieval
world map with all its misshapen

continents rolling off edges.
Our garden used to be an olive grove

miles wide. Just this tree's left
which means just these flies

and that one toad. A year
with no fruit and I didn't even notice.

Though I know how raw
olives taste bitter, the bark and leaves too.

The Mystery of Tides

In a star starved night, the big bone
colored moon mimics a severed head
of a horse, just one of its ghostly eyes

visible. Georgia O'Keeffe painted
such fleshed animal fragments, gigantic
flowers found in deserts, explaining

with shade and shape what she couldn't
with words. She'd understand
this moon. Just yesterday I read

engineers invented a buoy
able to convert the ocean's up
and down motion into enough

electricity to ignite every light
in Jerusalem. Yet if we steal
from the sea, what becomes penniless?

It makes sense — this fear
we'll drain the waves of their lift
their low, that the big waters, endless

from just about any perspective,
will flatten. No one's been able to find
what's hiding inside O'Keeffe's flowers.

So stop talking about this moon.

A Scent of Oranges

Up against the Yemenite quarter, market alleys
        slow as winter's early dusk closes them down.
Only the edges froth as the last customers grab
        what seems most necessary.

Kol kakh belegan — so much mess,
        kesef ketan — so little money,
an old man mutters, untumbling mounds
        of unsold oranges and sliced watermelons.

It takes fifty liters of water to grow
        an orange that fills the palm of a hand.
Oh God, I'm stupid with hunger,
        as hunger is stupid with the scent of halva,

sweet baklava, souring bread, and zattar.
        I can't make sense of any of it.
Only a few winters ago, an Arab boy exploded
        with three others in the market.

Now the storefronts quietly lock, customers
        carry their groceries home. The old man flips
open his radio, begins to shimmy. He hands me
        an orange. I peel it, breathing in the scent.

Field Guide to Mushrooms

Israel is a poisonous mushroom planted in the Arab garden
with the aim of sowing destruction, chaos, terrorism, and
crime in the Arab world.
> — Issam Dari, Editor-in-Chief
> *Teshreen* (a Syrian newspaper)

That's a simile built on bad
information. Just last summer, the grass
in our garden started dying in spherical patches
for no obvious reason. We'd forgotten
no tires or tubes, no tables or spools
that might have imprinted such Os.
The children said maybe the dog chasing his tail
trampled the grass though the dog's antics
are usually more random. On the Internet,
there were suggestions of fairies and elves or aliens,
whose pattering feet create, they say, paths
like those we've grown in our garden.
They go on: a ring in the field brings fortune
but to let your animals eat the grass is asking
for trouble. The gardener looked ill
when queried about the circles, and said
they result from a poisonous fungus he's trying
to kill. I asked why he's so certain? He replied,
Loesan, the Thai who works for him (who
even in the heat buttons his shirt
to the throat and likes climbing to the tops
of palms), gathered some of the small brown
mushrooms growing at the edge of the rings
in his pocket. He ate them with noodles
for lunch, thinking the mushrooms the same
as those his mother used to flavor
the Pad See-Ew back home. Within hours,

Loesan fell into a coma that lasted
almost a week. It took months to kill the fungus,
for the circles to clear. After checking
the *Field Guide to Mushrooms*, I wrote a letter
to the Syrian editor reporting
that Loesan had fully recovered,
the poisonous mushrooms in our garden
indigenous to Israel.

LAVENDER DOOR

During a 12-hour break in the rain,
the dumpy taupe house shaped like a toad
across the street
              disappears.
The man who lived in the house
five decades
              sits on my curb
drawing his toad house in shades of blue
and gold, an awning with Solomnic
                      columns
similar to the canopy designed
by Bernini for St. Peter's Basilica in Vatican
City
            except no dome.
Over the front steps, he sketches
a marble head of a god
                and a range of likenesses
of the Ptolemaic rulers.
Wasn't this what it looked like? he cries.
Just as I
          remember it, I tell him, except
for a lavender door.

EVERY NIGHT WITH VALENTINO

There's not light enough to fill
the face she wears or the small metal chair
alone in the garden from where
she watches television.

It's close to midnight
and a wind blows from the East,
loosing the leaves like static, loosing
her long gray hair, her caftan

unfastening. On cue, Valentino appears
on screen and her face
breaks open. He leans down
from his indigo horse as her eyes

shine back into his.
I may not be your first victim, he mouths,
*but by Allah, I shall be the one
you remember!*

Her Son of a Sheik, pomaded
and powdered, blows such eloquent
kisses. He will die
very young.

Call me Yasmin, she whispers,
sensing someone
watching. She rises and begins
to dance, arms akimbo

in the black and white
flicker of night. How girlish she looks
from a distance. All the doors
and windows of her house left open.

SIGHTHOUNDS

For Gai

My best friend wrote she's gone blind
in one eye, diabetes exploding
the small veins in her eyes. She loves chardonnay
and cake, said things
might get worse.
                    In the last world war,
one out of four planes shot down from the ground
were friendly. More on cloudy nights
when the radar failed. Tonight though, the sky
is clear, a full moon bleaching each corner
of garden.
            Even the shadows gleam,
and my small dog, foolish in the glow, barks
frantically.
                How immense the grass smells.

            My friend cuts out comics, sends them
with her letters. In one, Charlie Brown says:
Sometimes I lie awake at night, and ask myself,
Is this all there is?
                    What Charlie craves
my friend eats: sweet white wine, raspberry pie,
candy hearts, pancakes smothered in Karo
syrup. For that she trades away mere yellow,
takes her bite of cake.
                        She says blindness isn't
really black, it's transparent like a soft sun
through gauze. Only in dreams it's dark.
Then she hears planes pass by.
                            Sometimes clouds.

MARTINI WITH BORGES' EYES

They don't have the intimate easy touches of brothers
or lovers, yet their close conversation suggests
they've known each other a long time

perhaps childhood friends separated year
after year after one or the other moved
to London for work for a marriage

that's since ended. Now reunited over gin
and vermouth, the two forty-somethings, don't notice
how alike they've remained.

Each unconsciously mimes the other — thumbs hook
in the pockets of recently bought jeans, their heads
tilt in unison, then both nod,

one mouthing *right right right* as the other
says something agreeable, his lips forming words
I just make out through the bar's darkness —

*You know, Borges wasn't really blind, at least
not completely.* This stops me
and I search their winter pale faces

for something
like irony or wit, but they are each
intent on the other. If not blind

then what of Borges' hunger for libraries,
descriptions of books that in his poems smelled
of yesterday's rain. Though his fear

of mirrors suddenly seems rational — *I see no one
or some other self.* The two men stop speaking,
set down their Martini glasses. They hug

and I see how one clutches
the shirt of the other. Borges dreamed
the Ganges and of white tigers, their bones

heaving beneath covers
of skin, though later Borges admitted
his tigers were just symbols

like the word *blind*
like the two men, the darkness that wouldn't exist
but for these unreliable instruments, eyes.

Hind Leg of a Dog

A little girl lived in a red brick ranch house at the end of a cul de sac. She resembled all other little girls except for a birthmark on her left breast in the shape of a bud. For eight years, the flower blossomed on her body the color of pink agate and, from its center, the scent of just cut grass. She won't say

what happened, but sometime before she turned nine, the mark grew into what seemed to her a small animal, a toad or a half crippled dog, and at night it moaned, its breath reminding her of old meat or what's under a rock after a rain. She would wake, a hand to her mouth, to see a dog slouch out the half-closed door, dragging useless legs behind it.

One night, the birth mark shriveled into the shape of an eye shut, a red scar with lashes. The dog disappeared. She won't say

what happened. Not to worry. She kept quiet. She made sure the knife she returned to the kitchen was very
very clean.

STORIES OF SNAKES

The snakes don't come for the warmth
of humans though the smaller do crawl
close to our fires, along the ledges
of open lit windows. The rustle of mice

nibbling our old photos and unsent letters
entices them. An Egyptian myth holds
that in unwatched fields, a kind of thistle grows
red buds, afterwards blue flowers,

the stem's skin resembling
the most dangerous viper. Yet just one drop
of its juice turns even the deadliest venom
into sugar, while the dreams of grown women become
those of their children —.

What do you see, my mother asked
when I looked in her hand mirror. At my feet,
discarded bandages like snakes
unzipped from my own skin. But they weren't
real snakes. The viviparous young

camouflaged in branches, drowsing
amongst the blowsy hibiscus —
pale green anodyne — their fangs emerge
so slowly. I said to my mother,

I see a human girl. But my mother knew
newborn snakes don't dream
of our flesh, they dream
of flying. As only an accident stripped
them of wings.

NIRVANA

I've reached the road sign that reads Nirvana.
The turnoff is just ten kilometers north
of Tiberias, the Sea of Galilee. I gaze down
a gray gravel road that vanishes
into twisted rows of olive trees. They say it's where Jesus
walked on water, the obsidian lake gleaming
more solid than the mottled shore.

I want to believe it's possible to drive
to wisdom, that behind the ten shekel a night
campsites, the air-conditioned buses bursting
with Bible toters from Mumbai,
Miami, Milano, behind their tour-guided fervor
there's order. I want to believe zeal
is a rhyme for the real.

Right now, Nirvana seems lost
among the crushed cans, disposable cameras —
the refuse of too many pilgrims and fanatics.
A soft dusk begins to deepen the giant lake.
On the far edge, a father throws his child
into the water, then another, all three yelling
for more, the echo of their ecstasy clean
of churchy magic, flesh and flailing.

Notes Taken at Noon to Birdsong

Jerusalem sits among seven hills, stepped stone structures, each one
the height of several men.
Terraces of olive, terraces of almond, of date and fig.
Flocks of sparrows, clean water trickling from slits
in rock formations.

Once, an imprint of a shell.

> *The chirping*
> *is not in the least malicious.*

The Biblical Jews adopted certain customs of their enemies.
They inscribed the names of opponents on pottery
then smashed them, acting out
their destruction.
On the front lines, the blind and lame cast spells on attackers.

After the fighting, prisoners are arrayed naked in ranks, hands tied
behind. They stand still as a battalion of statues.

> *Their hearts aren't heavy*
> *even when they peck at a worm.*

The same Mediterranean. It's the same Mediterranean.
Poets write of it as of a just-spent lover, reminiscing
about its soft embrace.

"The sands of Jaffa, fine as ash."

A bridal dress from Ramallah with red beads and intricate embroidery.
Bracelets on the hands, ring in the nose, a veil edged in gold.

During the fifty days of *khamsin*, no bride sleeps.
Its grit in their teeth.

> *Some are rare, some common,*
> *but every wing is grace.*

Deaths in Damascus continue.
A senior advisor responsible for ferrying arms to terrorists
had returned with his wife to his seaside villa after a wedding.
The news from Jerusalem an assassin.
The news from Cairo suicidal.
No news from Damascus, or of his wife.

> *This chirping is entirely free of malice.*

In Jerusalem, bodies are buried one on top of another.
On each new slab, small pebbles in pyres. The weight, they say,
prevents the dead from escaping.

Road construction turns up ancient graves every day.
Sometimes it's difficult to tell which are remains of Jews,
which not.

All of them reburied, most carefully.

> *It even seems to have*
> *a note of compassion.*

THEIR CITY

Stairs made of stone that lead up
through walls washed yellow, pocked
as if by hundreds of moths,
the windows all undone.

A curtain of absolute white fluttering
over dark-scarved women who slowly ascend, descend
children in hand to mikvah, to market.

All at once, I've crossed some threshold —
this city
a place of unimaginable simplicity.

Just one moment more
I'll be lost.

EL AL FLIGHT 8

Clouds drift like sand in low tide as heads
      of children turn down, reading books, their mouths
moving. No sound but a throb of plane. It's 8 a.m.

      where I'm going. You've walked the dog, set
today's newspaper by a cup, and when I arrive home,
      it will seem as though I've just woken up.

Three seats in front of me, an Orthodox man
      stands, and through the dark, his soft prayer
reaches me: *Blessed are You, O Lord — shelo asani eesha —*

      who did not make me a woman. I shout out
at the man from a sleeping-pill dream. He sports
      a black coat, a black hat. The man I shout at

shouts *Draw!* Just *no bleeding Jesuses*
      you joked when I put up the tree in my office
last Christmas, then taught your daughter

      to sing Jingle Bells and Rudolph
in English. Yet there's tenderness
      in the way his wife moves his pillow from the seat

as he finishes his prayer. There are moments
      in line for the bathroom at a bar when I get
the man's point. Such nonsense! No sense

      of how the thing said is the words, how the words
are themselves the thing said. She has a self
      he rejoices in not knowing. I'm writing

a love poem: cup, transatlantic, gun fight,
          all those mouths moving, our hands swimming
beneath sheets, his back a mirror.

DREAMING OF JESUS

The church smells of old book. It's recently rained inside, or perhaps there's been weeping. As I enter, stained glass men irritably exchange place, long pews washed up from some Roman ship shift uncomfortably, clear their wooden throats. A bearded man I used to know awakens, muttering panic, slaps out a small fire erupting from his pocket. It's *delicious*, he whispers, stroking a thin red snake curled in his palm. I've returned, proving how quickly resolve decays in air, searching for an antidote or at least a sign. But the angels carved white with folded faces stare straight ahead, eyes unmoved. Outside, the sparrows remain in character and clouds hang open-ended. The bearded man, now dressed in a smoking jacket, takes my hand: *Every year it grows more subtle,* he says, *but in the end, it might give you a kiss.*

THE BEAUTY OF HOLES

If I stand still even long enough grass will grow
into me invisible
mites bite
        the foot's
sole

the first to disintegrate which might be one way
of settling
in
     so that I'll be *please god*
not

just a visitor
              and while vines thread their small hands
      through mine
dark roots will find their ways
to crevasses

I'll begin to live so low

as to have a name in
               the greenery

there's so much I've been wrong about

the earth's first days weren't nearly
so hot the sun
           putting out a third less energy
       which means windows

for living
        opened earlier just as it's not some irresistible
force that
ripped you and me

        faster apart
I mistook the slam of a car
             door for gravity
didn't dig heels in
      stand still

Everyday History

Violent clashes between Jewish and Arab residents of Akko
erupted when an Arab resident of the Old City drove through
a predominantly Jewish area on the eve of Yom Kippur.

If history must be made every day, let it be one in a car with all four windows rolled down, on the way to stay in a hotel built from the bones of what used to be a fortress. Let it be where the air is pomegranate sweet, where grass grows the color of crayon on parapets buried six inches deep in loam and fertilizer. If history must be made every day, let it be in a place where metal shutters don't function, where polyester pillows stuffed in windows muffle men singing karaoke in Arabic and Hebrew well enough for sleeping, where the only museum refuses to display anything airport security might confuse with a weapon. Let it be one where locals gather on carpets to eat hummus and salad, whistle at women (especially those wearing caftans, brightly patterned scarves) and the women understand that if one of them walked up, history might be made even that day. If history's got to be made, let it be the place where every one-legged policeman gets paid, where cats crouch in the shadows waiting for scraps they know are coming their way, any second.

WE ARE JOYOUS

Unchecked, at least for this moment
we roam the park, hooded crows, a spill
of motor oil until nothing
but a thin blade
remains of water's edge.

It's toward this silence Noah
launches his two last crows
and they must find shore, which is why
they don't return —

Still, I say, they are joyous.
They stay through winter feeding on
cat food, the bodies
of foolish pigeons falling
to their touch, like you

who takes a broom
to the two dull doves nested
on the ledge outside our
bedroom window, sweeping
them into air.

Looking for Jerusalem

I.

Twilight turns dry hills watery
green, the deserted fruit stand at the exit
transparent, as cars float above

on streets called desert flowers (Shoshan,
Vered, Rakefet), Mevaseret's miniature
bungalows rolling up and up

to Jerusalem. Almost delicate
the undulating barrier, its towers
electrified, marking Israel's western edge.

I stretch my head out the open window
hoping the view will fill me
with ideas of permanence,

love. I'll smell the immaculate stream
of history. All there is
is what the river drags (fish bones, frogs,

cigarette butts), the scummed surface
hardly parting as I sail through. No ripening
but my own strange life.

II.

My husband and I have been arguing
for kilometers about who are worse, Israeli
drivers, whose version of yielding
doesn't involve other vehicles, or Italians

where a persistent near miss is a kind
of kiss. Both consider blinkers a sign
of fragility, we agree. But I think
what we're really still arguing about

is reverence. It goes back to an earlier
quarrel, that one about a six lane
super highway built through the center
of a second century Jewish

cemetery, about the old Jewish bones
excavated on television
with meticulous religious attention
that have since gone missing.

It's wicked, I said, taking the side
of the misplaced remains. He defended
the living. Time, he tried to tell me, rides
two different trains. The first train

goes slowly, stops at every possible
station, the names of travelers, the minutia
of their belongings carefully noted. The second
travels at breathtaking speed.

It doesn't decelerate until
it reaches its destination, the people
on platforms an indistinguishable blur.
The first train, he said, *is hell. The second,*

heaven. It's only now, I ask,
For whom is it heaven —
the passengers or those watching them
race by?

III.

Everything's a sign.
Last spring, my sister-in-law
and her husband began

renovating their cellar,
creating room
for a second child. In the diggings

they found fragments of
pottery, what might
have been bones. After a brief

debate, they replaced
the shards, the dirt, decided to
add another floor to the roof.

Everything's
a sign, they said, *but only if*
you want it to be.

REVENGE

I ask myself — why yield so soon
to catastrophe, to the heartbreak
of headlines? Take Iphigenia —
in one version of the Greek
tragedy, she flourishes. In another,
she disappears.
Either way, the boats belonging
to her father laid waste
to Troy. The ending
the same for everyone
except Iphigenia.

I'm no sucker, says the girl
to the soldiers as she unfastens
the front of her dress, allows the vest
packed with explosives
to be taken. Her wide open eyes
find the television
cameras. Somewhere a gunship
wallows. Inside, a man watches
TV, wipes the ring left
by the glass from which he was
just drinking.

MILK INSIDE

I wake, having lost track
of the hours, a woman in the seat
next to me weeping
delicately, the thin
blue current of her shoulders
almost indistinguishable
from the shudders of the plane.
I'm not usually like this, she says,
shifting eyes from mine
to the window. I tell her, *At times,*
we are all like this, turning
to the book in my lap.
What I want to tell her is,
Stop. I've grown so impatient
with misery. In the book, a man
descends thirty-six thousand feet
below sea level to stare
at the deepest spot of the world.
Through his tiny portal cracking
under the enormous pressure
of ocean, he says the snuff-colored
ooze at the bottom resembles
a big bowl of milk. We think
we know misery
yet can't speak eloquently
of even such a visible chasm.
Inside this plane, nothing happens.
We are hundreds of miles
off course, our shape we recognize
only by the shadow
following. The woman stares out
the window, waiting for something
that won't come. She rises

then sits back down.
What I mean to tell her is,
Keep going.

THIS PLACE, FOR NOW

It's there, where the Yarqon River begins
— just a day's walk from its end at the sea
by a bend so broad the waters appear

stopped. On the banks, crowds of water lilies
crawl down, their soft baby heads trembling
in the air as if waiting to be born.

Twenty years ago, the water so foul
the lilies abandoned the dark river.
Last spring, they returned. I suppose all things

are provisional. Still I've grown weary
of starting over, weary of learning
landmarks and language, explaining myself

to men whose faces I won't remember.
This place marked a crossroad between Egypt
and Damascus. On the hill, a fortress

built by Sultan Salim falls down on what
remains of King Herod's walls. Somewhere near,
the Philistines defeated the Jews, took

their Ark. I say, *Good riddance.* The lilies
nod and beneath an oblivious blue,
we're running with the river toward the sea.

NOTES

"Living with Spiders." St. Thomas, also called Doubting Thomas, was one of the Twelve Apostles of Jesus. In Thomas' best known appearance in the New Testament (John 20:24-29), he doubts the death and resurrection of Jesus and demands to touch Jesus' wounds before being convinced.

"Bathsheba Poems." *Bathsheba at Her Bath* is an oil painting of the Biblical figure Bathsheba by Rembrandt Harmenszoon van Rijn (July 15, 1606 – Oct. 4, 1669) probably completed in 1654. Rembrandt was a Dutch painter and etcher and is considered one of the greatest painters in European art history. The model for Bathsheba was Rembrandt's partner Hendrickje Stoffels, who at the time was likely pregnant with their child. In Rembrandt's painting, a nude young woman sits on a white-draped bench, a letter in her hand. Lost in thought, she looks down as an elderly maidservant with an Oriental-style headdress washes her feet. David is not depicted. At the time of this book's publication, the painting hung in Room 11 of the Louvre Museum in Paris, France.

The Old Testament of the Bible contains two important episodes that relate to Bathsheba:

1. Bathsheba and King David (2 Samuel 11:1-26, 12:15-25): Bathsheba was seen by King David as she bathed, who requested that she come to him and lie with him. Subsequently, she became pregnant by him. Her husband Uriah, an important general in David's army, was intentionally sent to his death by David. Bathsheba then married the King. Her baby died. She had a second son, who was called Solomon.

2. Solomon takes the throne (1 Kings 1:1-37, 2:10-25): David lost his political clout in old age and the next in line for the throne had to be named. In a palace coup, Bathsheba and her adviser Nathan secured the throne for Solomon, even though there was an older brother,

Adonijah, who expected to succeed David. When Solomon took the throne, Bathsheba became Queen Mother, the most prestigious position a woman could hold. Bathsheba later took part in events that led to the execution of Adonijah, who was likely perceived as a continuing threat to Solomon.

"Notes Taken at Noon to Birdsong." Italicized lines are from Dahlia Ravikovitch's poem, "The Sound of Birds at Noon."

"El Al Flight 8." The line, "No sense of how the thing said is the words, how the words are themselves the thing said," is quoted from James Schuyler's poem, "Morning of the Poem."

"Milk Inside." The book referenced in the poem is *Seven Miles Down*, which was written by Jacques Piccard. Piccard was a Swiss engineer and explorer and one of only two people (as of 2010), along with Lt. Don Walsh, to have reached the deepest point on the earth's surface, the Challenger Deep, in the Mariana Trench. Their dive occurred in 1960.

ABOUT THE AUTHOR

Sarah Wetzel is a poet, essayist, and engineer. She grew up a daughter of the American South, but ended up in Israel after job-hopping across the Americas and Europe. Sarah graduated from Georgia Tech in 1989, and in 1997, received a MBA from The University of California, Berkeley. Despite both, Sarah completed a MFA in Creative Writing from Bennington College in January 2009. Sarah currently divides time between Israel and Manhattan, where she lives with her husband, four step-children, and one needy dog.